Confidence

Ultimate Self Confidence Discover How To Increase Your Self Confidence And Reach Your True Potential

By Ace McCloud

Copyright © 2014

Disclaimer

The information provided in this book is designed to provide helpful information on the subjects discussed. This book is not meant to be used, nor should it be used, to diagnose or treat any medical condition. For diagnosis or treatment of any medical problem, consult your own physician. The publisher and author are not responsible for any specific health or allergy needs that may require medical supervision and are not liable for any damages or negative consequences from any treatment, action, application or preparation, to any person reading or following the information in this book. Any references included are provided for informational purposes only. Readers should be aware that any websites or links listed in this book may change.

Table of Contents

Introduction 6
Chapter 1: The Basics of Self-Confidence 8
Chapter 2: The Mental Game—Habits to Boost Self-Confidence 11
Chapter 3: Goal Setting and Planning 16
Chapter 4: Building Self-Confidence Through Daily Actions 20
Chapter 5: Putting Self-Confidence Into Practice 26
Conclusion 30
My Other Books and Audio Books 31

Be sure to check out my website for all my Books and Audio books.

www.AcesEbooks.com

Introduction

I want to thank you and congratulate you for buying the book- Confidence: Ultimate Self Confidence- Discover How To Increase Your Self Confidence And Reach Your True Potential."

Do you sometimes find it difficult to make your own decisions? Are you constantly trying to be a perfectionist? Does criticism make you want to crawl under your blankets and waste away? Is your past holding you back, shaming you, and making you feel worthless? Could you just use some practical techniques to boost your confidence in key situations?

Self-confidence is a key factor in living a happy, successful, and fulfilling life. When you have a high sense of personal value, self-worth, and self-respect, your control over your life tends to be much better. People who have a good sense of control over their lives tend to be generally more happy, more motivated, more successful, and more content with their lives. Unfortunately, there are many people in this world who have low self-esteem—they feel no personal value, no sense of self-worth, and worst of all, they do not respect themselves.

When you have a low level of self-confidence, your tendency to talk to yourself negatively increases dramatically. You are the most important person in your life, so when you treat yourself badly and tell yourself that you are not worthy or deserving of great things, you are hurting yourself the worst. Negative self-talk can lead to some very bad habits. It can cause you to become overly critical of yourself and others, it can lead to constant worrying, anxiety, and depression, it can lead to a decline in your personal appearance and hygiene, and it can even cause you to lie to yourself and others, one of the worst habits possible if you're trying to have a great life.

In addition to those bad habits, low levels of self-confidence can cause you to shift the blame on other people rather than yourself, it can lead you to make excuses, and it can inhibit your ability to express your true feelings. All of these habits can be very detrimental in both your personal and work life. Finally, one of the biggest signs of having low self-confidence is that you are dependent on others. While having healthy relationships in your life is important and nurturing, the most important relationship you should have is with yourself. You're in the driver's seat when it comes you your life. When you're dependent on others, you can easily lose control and miss out on tremendous opportunities.

Does any of that sound like you? If so, you've picked up the right book to help yourself make one of the biggest and most important changes in your life. This book contains proven steps and strategies on how to combat those bad, confidence-killing habits so that you can bring out the best of your abilities. The information and exercises contained in this book are aimed to help you learn how to laugh, love yourself, surround yourself with the right people, and how to lessen your need for materialism. Most importantly, you can learn how to conquer your fears and embrace new experiences while bringing your confidence level to an all-time high!

Chapter 1: The Basics of Self-Confidence

Self-confidence is a personal attitude that goes hand-in-hand with having a positive and realistic outlook on yourself. When you have a high level of self-confidence, you tend to have better control over your life, a better ability to trust your own senses, and a better ability to believe in yourself. On that note, do not mistake having a high level of self-confidence for having the ability to do *everything*. The key to remember is that having lots of self-confidence requires being realistic—so even when you cannot reach a goal or get something accomplished, you can still maintain a positive outlook.

One more important thing to remember is that self-confidence is not often consistent—most of the time, there will be an area of your life that you may *not* be confident in (for example, you might not have much confidence in your math skills or your personal appearance) but that is okay. Often times, people figure out how to develop their confidence in other areas as they grow and mature. Everybody is different and your self-confidence plan may be different than someone else's.

What Determines Self-Confidence?

Many different factors contribute to your current level of self-confidence. When you're a child, the way your parents interact with you can have a big influence on how your general level of self-confidence level turns out to be. If your parents were constantly criticizing you, making demands of you, or overprotecting you, you may find yourself feeling inferior, dependent, and unimportant as an adult. If your parents were accepting of the mistakes you made or encouraged you to be independent, then you probably have a higher level of self-confidence as an adult.

The kind of friends you keep can also be an influence on your self-confidence. If your friends tend to have low levels of self-confidence, their way of thinking can often rub off on you without much notice. For example, if your best friend constantly finds things that are wrong with him/her, you might start picking up the same bad habit. If you are ambitious but your friends aren't, they might hold you back from taking on great opportunities, even if they don't realize it. For example, they might put you down when you mention going after a great goal. If you think that your friends are negatively affecting your self-confidence, you don't have to cut them off—instead, just become more aware of what's happening and have a chat with them. Let's face it, however, there are some people that are just plain old negative on a consistent basis with all sorts of bad things happening around them. In cases like this, sometimes you really need to ask yourself if you really need this person in your life. It will be much easier to boost your self-confidence and think independently if you surround yourself with uplifting and positive people and try and distance yourself from those people who may consciously or subconsciously be sabotaging your success potential.

A Foundation for Self-Confidence

You're may be reading this book because you aren't happy with where your current level of self-confidence lies or if you just want that extra boost of confidence that will really bring you to the next level. In just a few short pages, you will discover all sorts of effective strategies and tips to help you get yourself to where you want to be. For now, however, I want to share with you the secrets to building a great foundation for self-confidence. Like the foundation of your house, your foundation for self-confidence can serve as your starting point—as you read through the tips and strategies in this book, you can start building yourself up from there.

First and foremost: strength training, exercising, and eating healthy are the core foundations for having great self-confidence. In fact, those three things are pretty much essential for living your life to the fullest in all areas—physical health, mental health, relationships, finances, habits, and overall success. When you're in tip-top shape all around, you will often find yourself more energized, better able to focus, more inspired, and more motivated. In turn, you will often pose a higher chance of feeling great about yourself.

Exercising and eating right go a long way when it comes to boosting self-confidence. Most importantly, it gives you more energy to put toward achieving your goals. When you're in the best of health, it often feels as if you *want* to keep improving yourself. Exercising and eating right can also help you live longer, have less health problems, and it can help you look amazing! Who *doesn't* want to feel like they look strong, healthy, and attractive? That is one area that many people do not have a lot of confidence in. Building this foundation can help you conquer a great area of low self-confidence and perform at much higher levels of excellence. For more detailed information on how to do this, be sure to check out my bestselling books: Ultimate Health Secrets and Ultimate Energy.

Many great American heroes have been able to use this core foundation for their success and high levels of self-confidence. Arnold Schwarzenegger and Cal Ripken are great examples. At one time, Arnold Schwarzenegger spent a lot of time on bodybuilding. By taking care of *his* body, he was able to overcome many challenges and obstacles in his life and eventually made it to America, where his he won the Mr. Olympia contest six times in a row and became one of the biggest movie action stars in the history of the world!

Cal Ripken, a former Hall of Fame and World Series winning Baltimore Orioles baseball player is also very inspiring. He helped shape the way offensive baseball players in the major league play today and he was known as the "Iron Man" for playing 2,632 games in a row at a high level for over 16 years! His determination and self-care allowed him to go on to retire a hero (I was at his last game and the celebration was incredible!) and he continues on in retirement to do charity and help others get into the passion of being healthy and playing baseball. In a few chapters, you will read all about how *you* can use self-confidence to do great things like these two men.

Are you ready? Are you excited? Let's go!

Chapter 2: The Mental Game—Habits to Boost Self-Confidence

Your daily habits often have a major influence on your current level of self-confidence. When you have mostly bad habits, such as eating junk food or not taking care of your personal hygiene, your level of self-confidence will probably be very low. Habits are unconscious, every-day actions that you usually engage in without thinking much about them, so they tend to just happen naturally. So when you have too many bad habits, they can often take over your life and your self-confidence will probably not change for the better. The key is to move the opposite way—from bad habits to good. The good news is that there any many, *many* good habits to learn that can help you boost your self-confidence *and* they're easy to learn!

How to Quickly Learn Self-Confidence-Boosting Habits

There are many easy ways to get into the habit of something new. Everybody's personal strategy will be different. However, there are many ideas to choose from. You could leave reminders to yourself (for example, posting a note on the fridge reminding yourself that you aren't eating badly anymore). You could make your habit the first thing you do when you wake up (for example, if your personal hygiene is bad, start taking a shower first thing every morning). You can mentally prepare yourself and be specific in the changes you are going to make.

Most importantly, never give up! This principle not only goes for learning new habits but it is also important in being generally self-confident. The ability to be self-disciplined and having a strong sense of willpower is important for staying in control of your life. Most of the hard work goes on in your head—it's the mental game. When you have mastered the ability to be self-disciplined, your chances of staying confident can remain high. When you're self-disciplined, you won't let what other people say bring you down. You won't let *anything* affect your self-confidence. You can be in charge of it, all day, every day.

To become a master of self-discipline, you must first learn willpower. Willpower is the ability to resist instant gratification in exchange for reaching your long-term desires. Not only can willpower help you boost your self-confidence but it can also help you reach goals in other areas of your life, which is priceless. The best way to learn willpower is to practice it. It's just like a muscle—the more you use it, the stronger you will become. For an in-depth guide on how to exert willpower and self-discipline, please see my other book Influence, Willpower and Discipline. To get the maximum results in self-confidence from reading this book, I highly recommend that you pause for a moment and check out this book, as it can greatly supplement you in this journey.

Now, onto the habits that can help you boost your self-confidence! Some of these habits are core habits, meaning that they can help you in other areas of your life as well! These core habits are especially valuable to make a part of your everyday routine.

Habits to Boost Self-Confidence

80/20 Rule. Knowing how to use the 80/20 rule to your advantage is an important, core habit that you should learn before trying out any of the next couple of habits. Basically, this rule suggests that you should focus on the most important 20% of what you're working on to increase your peak results by 80%. This is a powerful technique that can help you in all areas of life, not just with self-confidence, so it is important to know what 20% of the task to focus the majority of your attention on.

Visualization. Visualization is another core habit that is a very powerful and useful technique. When you practice visualization, your chances of achieving a goal that you have been thinking and visualizing about can increase dramatically. By visualizing yourself having already achieved your goal, you can use the feel-good vibes to increase your chances of actually accomplishing it. Be as specific as you can in your visualizations—think about how you'll feel, what you'll look like, what you'll touch, what you'll smell, etc. It's also a good idea to visualize yourself accomplishing all the steps that will lead up to your goal, and using a far away "camera angle" can increase the effectiveness of visualization.

Exercise. As I mentioned earlier, getting into the habit of exercise is crucial for building the foundation of having a high level of self-confidence. Exercising can keep you healthy and in shape and it is great for fending off mental stress. It is an overall feel-good activity that can keep you feeling confident and ready to take on the world. A good exercise regimen should include some warm-up exercises, some cardio, some strength training, and then some cool down exercises. For an in-depth, specific exercise plan on cardio and strength training exercises, I highly encourage you to check out my other book, [Ultimate Health Secrets](#), which can help you build up your underlying health foundation. It contains everything you need to know about eating healthy, supplements, the food pyramid, how to plan your meals, and it also includes an instructional guide on how to master some of the best workouts. The healthier you are, the more successful you can be in achieving a high level of self-confidence!

Think About Your Good Qualities. By focusing on the qualities about yourself that are good, you can help yourself gain a high level of self-confidence. For example, if you're about to give an oral report and you're nervous, but you know that you're a very organized person, focus on that and your chances of doing great can be bigger.

Reflect on Positive Experiences. Many people with low self-esteem tend to wallow on negative past experiences. By thinking about times when you felt your greatest, you can use those examples to push forward into the future. For example, think about a time when you made a great accomplishment at work.

Remember how good it felt and what you did to get there. Your chances of feeling more confident in the moment can increase. It's also a good idea to make a journal and record of all your favorite positive experiences that you have had throughout your life. You can include pictures, awards, events, friends, anything else that makes you happy. Then, be sure and read through this journal a couple of times a week to keep your spirits high.

"Stop" Negative Thoughts. Learn how to become more aware of when you start thinking negatively and then say "stop," either out loud or internally. Many therapists use this technique and you can do it yourself, anywhere. This can prevent you from getting too wrapped up in negative emotions that can bring down your self-confidence. To learn some awesome and easy do-it-yourself techniques on how to stop thinking negatively, I invite you to check out this YouTube video by Nathanaiel Solace: Negative Thoughts: How to Stop Negative Thoughts, Fear, Stress & Self Doubt.

Be Thankful. Be thankful for the things that you *do* have as opposed to thinking about the things that you *don't* have. When you think about things that you want, your mind tends to start focusing on your weaknesses that prevent you from having those things. By being thankful, you can live more positively and you can feel it more in your confidence. Try and list thirty things that you are thankful for each day.

Practice Good Posture. When you slouch or slump over, you are essentially sending a message to other people that you have low self-confidence. In turn, that could deter people from approaching you and you may start to feel less confident in being social. When you practice good posture, such as standing tall and strong, it shows that you are proud of yourself and it may make you more approachable. When you stand tall, it helps you feel important internally. Be sure to practice making eye contact and keeping your head up, too. For a good video on how to practice good posture, check out this helpful YouTube video by Posture Confidence, How To Get Good Posture.

Dress Well. The way you dress often says a lot about you and can influence how you feel about yourself. By dressing well, you can make yourself look even better than you already are and you can feel more empowered. Although it may feel like others judge you by the way you dress, the person who judges you the most tends to be yourself. That being said, you don't have to dress up in a suit or tie every day. Just try to avoid wearing dirty, wrinkled, ripped, or old clothing. Look presentable and well groomed.

Be Heard. People who have low levels of self-confidence tend to stay quiet when they are in large groups. This usually happens out of a fear of being judged. However, it is important to remember that not everybody is as judging as you think! Even by just speaking up once or twice every time you're around people, you can help yourself get better at public speaking, which can really help you become more confident. For some very helpful tips on improving your public speaking skills, check out the informative YouTube video called "How To Speak Up Without Freaking Out", posted by Dice News. It's aimed toward public speaking at work but you can always apply the principles to other situations.

Make Contributions. Making contributions to other people and projects can be a great way to become more confident. You could donate old clothes, volunteer your time, give some food, mentor a child, or anything else you can think of. When you lend your service to others, it generally helps you feel better about yourself, knowing that you helped out somebody who is going through a rough time.

Get to Know Yourself. Knowing yourself and what you like is a major way to become more confident. When you know yourself, what you want, what you like, where you want to be, etc, you can have a better sense of control over your life. A good way to get to know yourself better is to engage in some alone time. A good idea may be to start a journal, where you can pour out your deepest thoughts.

Live By Your Values. Most people have core values, such as family, religion, morales, etc. Your values serve as another foundation of how you make decisions in life. Live by your values and make the decisions in the best light that reflects your values. This can help you become more fulfilled and confident in the long-run. For a better idea of core values and some examples, check out the informative YouTube video called "What Are Personal Core Values", posted by values test quiz.

Don't Talk Fast. When you speak quickly, you can give off the impression to others that you feel like your thoughts don't matter. When you speak slowly, you tend to come off as more of an authoritative figure. Speaking slowly can also help you become more clear and communicative, which can have positive effects on your social life.

Stay Educated. When you keep yourself educated, your chances of being able to have intelligent conversations with people highly increases, which can help you feel more confident. If you're no longer in school, you could always study a topic by picking up a good book or doing some internet research. You could even just read the newspaper each morning to stay on top of trending topics. By doing this, you'll always have something to talk about.

Set and Achieve Small Goals. By setting and achieving small goals, you can build your confidence up to the point where you feel ready and able to take on bigger and more long-term goals. You can even make it easier to accomplish a long-term goal by breaking it down into short-term goals. A great idea is to always start your goal off with the phrase: "I will easily..."

Meditate. Meditation is a powerful way to help yourself engage in your thoughts and learn how to control them. Meditation is easy and you can do it anywhere, as long as you are comfortable with what you're wearing and you have a peaceful, quiet place to do it. It can be very refreshing for your mind and it can really help you harness your confidence. Check out two great YouTube meditations– "Boost Your Serotonin, Dopamin,e & Endorphin Release – Binaural Beats + Isochronic Tones," posted by Brainwave Power Music; and "Best Ever Gong Meditation May 20th 2013", posted by Gongster.

Good Music. Listening to positive and uplifting music can be great for your overall mood and wellbeing, thus increasing your confidence levels. Try and avoid negative music and instead focus on music that makes you happy and energetic. Here is one of my favorite music cd's: Fairy in the Woods, and you can find an incredible assortment of great music for free on YouTube. Here are a couple of my favorite YouTube videos to listen to while working at the computer: Creative Focus by Jason Lewis, Extremely Powerful Pure Clean Positive Energy by Brainwave Power Music, and Brain Music: Study Focus Concentrate by relaxingrecords.

Forgiveness. Being able to forgive is critical in order for you to be able to focus on more important things than the bad memories and trauma of the past. Although forgiveness can be extremely difficult, it can be one of the most important things you do for your overall mental wellbeing. For advanced knowledge on how to forgive, check out my book: Forgiveness.

Team Up With Confident Friends. When you surround yourself with other people who are highly confident, your chances of feeling more confident will likely go up. By surrounding yourself with other confident people, your chances of being surrounded by negative thoughts can dramatically decrease because there will be less judgment and jealously going around.

Be Humble. Avoid bragging and other ego-inflating activities. Be humble and modest and you can feel more confident. When you act this way, your confidence can naturally shine through you and you won't have to put so much effort into trying to impress others.

Hypnosis. In some cases, many people turn to hypnosis techniques to help them get a better grasp on becoming more confident. Hypnosis has been very effective for most people and it is definitely an interesting approach. You can give hypnosis a try by going to a professional or you can give self-hypnosis a shot. If you are thinking about giving self-hypnosis a try, I highly recommend starting out with the Quick Confidence Booster from hypnosisdownloads.com. If you find that hypnosis works for you, there are many more downloads to choose from at that site.

Chapter 3: Goal Setting and Planning

To help increase the likelihood that you will reach your maximum level of self-confidence, it is a good idea to understand the importance of setting goals. When you set a goal for yourself, your chances of actually reaching the end-result are often much higher because it requires a bit of planning and visualizing. Setting goals can help you stay on track to achieving your long-term goals.

Goals are important for several reasons. They help you define your expectations, track your progress, and stay motivated. When you set a goal, you should always make sure that your goal is measured out in specific terms, is realistic and attainable, and is measurable. That means that you should keep track of your progress by writing it down and regularly reviewing it. Always start with small steps, even if you're planning on achieving a long-term goal. Never stress yourself out, because that can actually decrease your chances of reaching your goal. Finally, always make sure that you have complete control over the end result.

This chapter will show you how to integrate goal-setting and planning into your life so that you can boost your self-confidence.

Goal #1: Know Yourself and What You Want

This goal is one of the most important goals you can ever set. If you don't know yourself and ultimately, what you want out of life, how will you ever get to it? For this goal, I want you to grab a piece of paper and draw a chart with four columns. Over each column, write one of these categories: strengths, personal abilities, physical abilities, and interests.

Under strengths, write down everything about you that you believe is strong about yourself. For example, you may write down that you are trustworthy and reliable. Under personal abilities, write down any of your natural talents. For example, if you're really good at remembering things, you might write down that you have a strong memory. Under physical abilities, write down any physical strengths that you have. For example, if you're an good video game player, you might write down excellent hand-eye coordination skills. Finally, write down your true interests in the last column. This can be anything from playing sports to reading, writing, working with computers, playing an instrument, or anything else.

Next, review your chart and set some specific goals for yourself based off the information you've come up with. For example, if one of your interests is to play the piano, you might want to make it a goal to become a piano teacher. There is no doubt that you'd love that job because of your love for the piano. See if you can set a goal for yourself based off of each category. By applying your strengths and talents to your life and career, you can become an expert at anything that you set your mind to and that in turn can really help boost your self-confidence.

Goal #2: Stay Motivated

When you're self-motivated, your level of self-confidence tends to be very high. Staying motivated helps you stick to your goals and it can make you feel great about yourself at the same time. The more motivated you are, the more confident you will likely be.

Take out your chart and pick one of your goals. Let's pretend that one of your goals is to become a professional runner. To stay motivated towards achieving this goal, you could make it a short-term goal to run for at least 40 minutes each day (as a bonus, exercise is great for boosting self-confidence!). Under each goal you've set for yourself, I want you to brainstorm some ways that you can stay motivated toward achieving each one. The more you work on each goal, the more confident you can feel as you come close to achieving them. For some more expert knowledge on getting yourself motivated, be sure to check out my book: Motivation.

Goal #3: Take Care of Your Body

As I have mentioned several times throughout this book, exercise and a healthy diet is the foundation for being confident. If your exercise and eating habits are not currently up to par, now is a great time to use some goal-setting and planning to change it. This can be a completely separate goal to achieve since it may be a huge change to some people. Do not try to jump into this goal all at once or you risk becoming too overwhelmed to the point where you might give up.

Diet. To start, take a new piece of paper or flip to the backside of your personal chart. Make two columns. On the right side, write down some thoughts on what your current diet is like. Do you eat breakfast every morning? Do you get enough whole grains? Do you tend to eat too much junk food? Do you drink enough water? Ask yourself those types of questions. In the left column, write down some thoughts on how you will change each bad eating habit. For example, if you eat too much junk food, make it a goal to start snacking on fruits and vegetables instead. By making small switches like that, you can work your way up to breaking all of your bad dietary habits.

Exercise. Again, make two more columns and now write down your current exercise habits in the right. Be sure to include bad habits, such as sitting on the couch or in front of the computer too much. In the left column, think of ways to slowly start breaking those bad habits. For example, if you work long days and you can't really make time to exercise, make small changes like parking your car far away or taking the stairs when you can.

A subcategory of this goal is your personal appearance and hygiene. As you may remember from Chapter 2, getting into the habit of taking pride in your appearance can have a profound effect on your level of self-confidence. This can be another separate goal that you can work on in small steps. Doing simple things like taking daily showers, brushing your teeth twice a day and wearing a nice-smelling perfume or cologne can make a big difference. When it comes to dressing well, research what colors look best on people with your skin complexion. You can also research the latest fashion trends and popular clothing brands. Most importantly, make sure it is something that you like and feel confident in. Finally, don't forget to top it all off with a smile!

Goal #4: Stay Confident With a Sharp Mind

When your mind is sharp, you tend to be much more knowledgeable and intelligent (which makes you a great person to have a conversation with) and your chances of wanting to challenge yourself tend to be much higher. Personal challenges can make your self-confidence go through the roof. When you don't challenge yourself to move ahead in life, you risk the chance of becoming one of those people who just waste away on the couch every night. People with sharp and clear minds have a much better chance of having high levels of self-confidence.

There are many great ways to keep your mind sharp and intact. You could make it a goal to read more, solve puzzles, play strategy games (such as chess), keep up on the latest news stories, play video games, keep a journal, read, or try learning a new word every day. One interesting thing you can do to keep your mind in the best shape is to start memorizing the names of everyone you meet. This is especially helpful in a career setting. As an added bonus, research shows that you become much more likeable when you remember the names of everyone you meet.

Goal #5: Regularly Evaluate Your Goals

Finally, never forget to review and evaluate your goals at least monthly, and ideally daily. By regularly assessing yourself and your progress, your chances of giving up can dramatically decrease and when you see yourself making progress, you can become more motivated to keep going.

Never give up! Staying consistent in your goals is so powerful. Your goals are what will help you improve every day so that you can move forward in life. Start by following these 5 goals and you will likely start coming up with more specific, personal goals on your own. By setting and achieving goals, you become great, happy, and confident. Most importantly, you'll feel motivated, which is another critical piece of foundation for self-confidence. Always remind yourself that you *can* and you **will** achieve your goals, no matter how long it takes or what obstacles come up. Remind yourself that you will be a professional! As long as you put great focus into your goals, you can be really amazed by the end-results! Developing a winning attitude of never giving up is what has allowed me to personally achieve many great things in my life. I don't care how many times I fail, if it is something that I am passionate about, I will just keep on trying, and eventually victory is attained. By not giving up, all the consistent victories begin to pile up, which make it much easier to feel confident. Many like to call this the "Winning Mindset" and it is what the greatest people throughout history have possessed.

Chapter 4: Building Self-Confidence Through Daily Actions

Good Relationships and Self-Confidence

You probably have many different relationships in your life. I've mentioned that your most important relationship is with yourself, but you can't forget about your loved ones, friends, and co-workers. People who have a high level of self-confidence tend to have better relationships than those who have a low level of self-confidence. When your relationships with others are good, your life can be much happier. When you do not have good relationships in your life, you can pose a risk of becoming isolated, lonely, depressed, and not likeable.

Your level of self-confidence also plays a role on how you influence the relationships that others have with *you*. When your self-confidence is low, you may have a hard time relating to others. It can affect your ability to socialize with groups of people. People will often be able to sense your low self-confidence through your body language. It is common for people to take advantage of you when they can tell that you are not very confident, so it is very important to maintain a high level of self-confidence. The good news is that when you have a high level of self-confidence, your relationships tend to be much better and healthier, so you do not have to worry about tending to your relationships that much.

How Are Your Relationships?

Before we get into this section, here is a brief questionnaire that you can use to evaluate the relationships in your life:

- Is it easy for you to speak up for yourself?
- Do you find yourself often feeling invisible or unappreciated?
- Do you put your own needs before the needs of others?
- Do you feel alone?
- Do you feel the need to be in control?
- Is it hard for you to trust?
- Do you want to generally improve your relationships?

Think about these questions for each of the important relationships in your life. For example, when it comes to your relationship with your parents, can you speak up for yourself without any problems? When it comes to your relationship with your boss, do you feel that you put his or her needs before yours? Take a moment to evaluate the most important relationships in your life before reading on. If you are dissatisfied with any of the answers, the rest of this section will aim to teach you how to improve your relationships with self-confidence.

Ways Confidence Can Strengthen Relationships

Healthy relationships of all kinds are usually composed of honesty, trust, and respect.

You Can Be Your Best. When you're a confident person, you usually also have a high level of self-respect. When you respect yourself, you tend to be a better friend and a better partner. Self-respect and confidence will help you realize that you deserve love and respect in return. When you display this attitude, the people in your life will be more likely to treat you in the same way. One example of how low self-confidence can negatively affect your relationships is when you and the other person do not respect each other. If you feel taken advantage of by somebody, it is usually a sign that you should work on building your self-confidence.

People Will Take You Seriously. When your self confidence is high, people will take you seriously. It can be easier for them to see your value and your true worth. It can also help you get your voice and ideas heard. It is important for both your friends and your partner to take you seriously, otherwise you may end up feeling worthless and depressed.

You'll Meet More New People. When you're confident, your ability to go up to strangers and start a conversation is most likely higher. When it's easy for you to talk to people, you can easily open the door to many new and exciting opportunities in your life. Whether you start talking to a cute girl at a restaurant or you start talking to a friend of a friend who turns out to have job opportunities, your chances of your life being more interesting and successful can go way up.

You'll Have Higher Standards. When you're confident, your relationship standards will likely be better. People with low self-confidence tend to surround themselves with similar friends. Sometimes these people can be drug users, freeloaders, or just plain lazy to the point where they don't even want to hold up their end of the relationship. High self-confidence allows you to pick and choose who you want to associate with. Likely, you will associate with those who are similar to you. When you surround yourself with successful people, your chances of being successful often becomes much higher.

You Won't Be Jealous. This is true especially in romantic relationships. When your self-confidence level is high, your chance of being a jealous and controlling partner can decrease. When you do not have confidence in a romantic relationship, the root cause is usually because you are not confident yourself. This personality trait often leads to relationship issues and ultimately breakups.

You'll Own Up. When you have a high level of self-confidence, your ability to own up when you're wrong can be much better. If you can admit when you are wrong in certain situations, it can make you a much more likeable and respectable person. Being able to own up can also prevent heated arguments, tension, and other relationship issues.

Building a Support System

Now that you have a better understanding about how confidence can affect your relationships, a good idea would be to start building a support system. Think of the most important people in your life, who can bring out the best in you, and make it a point to work with each other on building your self-confidence. When you have people to do it with, your chances of getting it done can be much higher. Try to think of one family member, one friend, and one co-worker who you can do this with. Remember; always surround yourself with positive, supportive people! Negativity spreads like wildfire and can bring down not only your confidence, but your ability to go after future opportunities. It's often said that "One bad apple spoils the bunch."

Your Finances and Self-Confidence

Have you ever looked at your bank statement and just wanted to cry? Of course, there's no way to get out of paying the cost of your living, which often takes up the majority of your paychecks and as you probably know, that alone can be very depressing. However, did you know that your self-confidence can have a direct impact on your finances?

Research shows that people with a high level of self-confidence can earn more money, be more successful, and have a better feeling of job satisfaction than those who are not confident. Now, that doesn't mean that you can increase your paychecks overnight just by boosting your self-confidence. However, it *does* mean that if you do continue to keep working on your confidence, your job opportunities may be better in the future.

If you have a low level of self-confidence, it can literally scare you away from reaching your full earning potential. For example, you might have a GREAT idea for a business. It could reach hundreds of thousands of people and earn you unlimited income. However, you might hear yourself saying, "But I don't have what it takes." When that happens, you'll most likely end up working a low-end job in which you exchange time for money. When you believe in yourself, however, you're more likely to say, "Wait, I can do that! I'm going to at least give it a shot." Healthy risk-taking is a great side-effect of high self-confidence.

If you're not the type of person to start a business and work for yourself, your level of self-confidence can make or break how far you get in the company that you work for. One good example is about people who work in fast food restaurants. Fast food restaurants have a stigma for being "teenage summer jobs," or "dead-end jobs" in which you'll never move up. However, if you believe in yourself and are willing to work hard, your chances of being able to move up can be much higher. Many confident people who become corporate successes started out at the bottom. The moral of the story is that the more you believe in yourself, the harder you're going to work and the more doors for success will be opening for you.

Music and Self-Confidence

Can you get through the day without music? Music is all around you—on the radio, in your phones, on the computer, and maybe even at school. It is often said that music is the language of the soul, since it can affect people without using any words.

One way to boost your self-confidence through music is to learn how to play an instrument. Playing a musical instrument is a fun and sometimes a social way to feel great about yourself. If you have to start from scratch and learn how to read music as well as how to operate an instrument, your confidence will likely go up once you've gotten really good at it. The satisfaction of learning how to play an instrument can really help you. The commitment you make to learning how to play it can also help you become more confident and instill useful time management and goal-setting skills as well. Once you've mastered your instrument, you can play for friends and family or team up with a band for some jam sessions.

Music can also have a very powerful effect on your mood. Happy, upbeat music tends to make you feel positive and energetic while you may prefer to listen to slower and softer music when you're sad. You might listen to some dark, heavy metal music when you're angry. If you're a writer, you might even express your feelings through your own song lyrics.

There are some songs with lyrics that can really influence your self-confidence. For example, if you need an inspirational burst of self-confidence, you could listen to a song such as "Can't Touch This" by MC Hammer, a fun and upbeat song about being confident. If you need to work on self-acceptance, you could listen to "Born This Way" by Lady Gaga, which sends the message that you should not be embarrassed about anything that makes you different. Some songs can even help you become more confident about your physical appearance, such as "Beautiful" by Christina Aguilera. There are so many songs that can help you boost your self-confidence, the possibilities are endless.

Here are some more songs that you can listen to, to get started:

"Happy" by Pharrell Williams

"Survivor" by Destiny's Child

"Greatest Love of All" by Whitney Houston

"True Colors" by Phil Collins

"You Are Loved" by Josh Groban

"Empire State of Mind" by Jay-Z

"Perfect" by Pink

"Beautiful" by Eminem

"Firework" by Katy Perry

"Titanium" by David Guetta

Be sure to keep your ears open for these songs and any other songs that you find help your own self-confidence, since everybody has different preferences. You can make playlists of your most favorite confidence-boosting songs and carry them around with you in your car, on your phones, on your music players, and listen to them anytime you're feeling down or discouraged.

Keeping a Journal and Voice Recording

One great way to keep track of all the positive things about yourself and your life is to keep a journal. When good things happen to you, write about them before you go to bed, while they're still fresh in your mind. Many peoples' lives are so busy and hectic that it can be easy to quickly forget about the positive things that happen in place of the negative things that happen. This way, you can go back and read about them any time you're feeling low. When you read about them and remind yourself of the great things that have happened to you, you can easily remember that you are worth so much. Try to only write about good things and avoid writing about any bad things, otherwise you will just refill your mind with negativity.

Your journal can be anything. It can range from a simple notepad or composition book to one with a pretty, fancy cover. The choice is yours. Keep it in a private place where nobody but yourself can read it. Make it fun, write in it with a pen that produces your favorite color. If you really want to be creative, fill it with inspiring pictures, fun stickers, or anything else that you can use to personalize it.

If you're not sure what to start writing about, start out with this: write down one thing that you did each day that made you feel good about yourself. Did you hold the door for somebody? Write it down. Did you offer to buy coffee for a friend? Write it down. Start out with that and see where it takes you. After a week or so, see if you notice any differences in how you feel about yourself.

Another good idea is to use a small voice recorder to record experiences right away. You could download the audio to your music player or computer and listen to it as a way to relax yourself. If you get into journal writing and find that it really works great for you and you end up filling multiple journals, you could make it a goal to condense the "best of" those journals into one. That way, you can quickly scan over all of the moments in your life where you were at your best.

Chapter 5: Putting Self-Confidence Into Practice

Now that you've learned how to harness the power of self-confidence, let's take a look at some ways you can put it into practice. This chapter will review some great confidence-boosting exercises as well as list the best foods to incorporate into your daily diet for staying confident. Finally, you will learn a little bit about herbal remedies and how they can help keep you feeling strong and confident.

Great Self-Confidence Exercises

Correct Interpretation. At some point in your life, you have probably been the butt of a bad joke. How did you feel? Angry? Hurt? There's nothing worse than having a bunch of people laugh at you and feeling embarrassed or bad about yourself. However, you can sometimes prevent feeling that way if you correctly understand where the insult was coming from in the first place. Many times, you will encounter somebody who is purposefully trying to hurt your feelings. On the other hand, you may have some friends and family members who just like to tease and be sarcastic. Usually, those types of people don't truly intend any harm.

For example, if you're wearing a bright orange shirt, a friend might joke that you look like you're ready to go direct traffic. Now, you're friend probably didn't mean that in a way other than to just try and be funny, but you might interpret it as a bash on your fashion sense. Research actually shows that people who are sarcastic and witty often mistakenly insult others because they do not think of the implications their jokes can have. If you are ever in a situation like that, the best thing to do would be to step back from the situation and ask yourself, "Does this person just have bad social skills?" or "Is this a situation that is okay for me to take lightly?"

Emotion and Problem-Focused Coping. Is it inevitable for you to avoid being around somebody who is constantly being negative? In many cases, you may find yourself stuck in this situation with a family member or co-worker, and it would be illogical to quit your job or stop interacting with your family just to avoid them. When that happens, you can use one of two techniques to help protect your self-confidence from being damaged. First, you could use emotion-focused coping, which can help you manage stressful, unavoidable situations. In cases where you can't avoid a negative person, remind yourself that their comments are a reflection of their own confidence, not yours. If that does not work, you can try problem-focused coping. With problem-focused coping, you can talk with the other person to try and address the problem. Sometimes, that still won't change the situation. However, it can give you a better sense of control over your own self-confidence.

Self-Talk. The way you think and talk to yourself can have a huge impact on how you act. One great way to boost your self-confidence is to learn how to talk to yourself in a way that can help drive you to make positive changes in your life. For example, if you are an introvert, you may think to yourself, "I am shy," when you're around groups of people. You probably feel nervous in those situations. In that case, you can change the way you talk to yourself to try and change your actions. For example, tell yourself how you *want* to be. Instead of saying, "I'm shy," tell yourself that you want to be friendly with others when you're in a group. By doing that, you may feel more encouraged to be interested in other people. You can apply this technique to any area of life in which you're not feeling confident. It's also a good idea to have a few favorite positive affirmations that you can think to yourself when you want to be more productive or just drown out any negative self-talk. A few examples of a positive affirmation is: "I am super strong, happy, healthy and happy." Or "I am extremely confident and people love me." Be sure to use some creativity, and come up with a few catch phrases that appeal to you and your goals.

Prepare Yourself for Pressure. In life, it is pretty much impossible to avoid situations in which you're put under pressure. Often times, you do not get much time to prepare for these situations. When these things happen, you may feel a blow to your confidence because you're not sure what to say or do. To avoid that and to protect your confidence, there are some things that you can do. One great technique is to plan out scenarios and how you're going to act. Here are some scenarios in which you can plan out what to think or say when you're in the moment:

1) When your boss puts a rush on a task and you have no extra time.

2) When a client or colleague who you are responsible for overseeing messes up.

3) When a loved one asks you for a favor that you don't want to do.

4) If one of your employees gives you endless excuses for making a mistake.

5) Any other peer-pressure moment that you may want to avoid based off your personal life.

Five Foods to Boost Self-Confidence

In addition to eating and maintaining a healthy diet, research has shown that there are five certain foods that are really good for helping you remain confident. These foods, which you will learn shortly, contain tryptophan, an amino acid which boosts the level of serotonin in your brain. Serotonin is a chemical in your brain that can help you feel good about yourself, therefore boosting your self-confidence. The higher the level of serotonin in your body, the less chance you have of feeling depressed.

Here are the five main foods that contain tryptophan:

Turkey. Turkey is one of the best foods you can eat to boost your serotonin levels. Have you ever felt relaxed and sleepy after a Thanksgiving dinner? The tryptophan is probably why. Turkey also contains many essential fats, which makes it an excellent food to add to your diet.

Salmon. Salmon contains a fat called DHA, which can help lessen any feelings of depression. You can also substitute salmon with other fatty fish, such as mackerel or sardines. If you don't like or are allergic to seafood, you can take a fish oil supplement instead, like [Omega-3 Fish Oil](#).

Leafy Greens. Leafy green vegetables, such as spinach, contain high levels of folic acid, which can help stabilize your levels of serotonin. In addition to leafy greens, you can also provide your body with folic acid by eating almonds, lentils, nuts, and dried beans.

Buckwheat. Out of all of the starchy food out there, Buckwheat has the highest count of tryptophan. Buckwheat also contains lots of Vitamin B, which can help boost your levels of serotonin.

Dark Chocolate. Dark chocolate with a cocoa percentage of 70% or higher can help boost your serotonin levels. As an added bonus, dark chocolate also contains many healthy antioxidants.

Common Herbal Medications for Self-Confidence

For centuries, plants have been known to be great natural remedies for many ailments. Herbal medicine is now available in both over-the-counter and alternative medicine options. One thing that can be treated with herbal medication is low self-confidence. Many people prefer to use herbal medication because it tends to have less side effects than traditional medicine. Before taking any type of medicine, you should always consult your doctor.

St. John's Wort. This medicine, a flowering herb, has been widely used to treat depression and anxiety as well as the symptoms of those two illnesses, such as sleeping trouble and loss of appetite. Many people use this herb as an alternative to anti-depressants. People who have a low level of self-confidence can sometimes be very depressed. This herb can be used to help reverse those feelings.

Ginkgo Biloba. This herb has also been used to treat depression, especially in those who are 55 and older. Specifically, this herb can stimulate circulation in your brain, which can help boost your serotonin levels.

Licorice Root. Licorice root, which contains double the sweetness of sugar, is best known for uplifting your mood. It can also help your body absorb serotonin. Licorice root serves as a great anti-depressant and can be excellent for boosting your self-confidence and energy levels. I personally take this supplement every day.

Ginseng. Ginseng, a herb that is famously known for being an ingredient in tea, is great for boosting your energy, which can in turn help you focus on becoming more confident. Ginseng also has many beneficial effects, such as boosting your appetite and preventing common colds.

Chamomile. Chamomile, another herb that is commonly found in tea, it is great for reducing anxiety and reducing excessive tiredness. When you're able to rest and relax, your ability to be more confident can be much higher.

Larch. Larch is a flower essence that is known to help those who are feeling depressed with low self-confidence. People who feel inferior and unsuccessful can many times benefit from using this essence. Many people have reported feeling more confident and determined after using larch.

Rock Rose. If you have experienced a serious illness or injury in the past, it is possible that it has made you fearful and panic-ridden, which can lead to having low levels of self-confidence. The flower essence Rock Rose has been known to help people become calm and more confident.

Cerato. If your self-confidence is low, you may have trouble with decision-making. The flower essence Cerato is known to empower people with the ability to trust in themselves and to trust in their common sense. Cerato has helped many people become more certain with their decisions.

Hornbeam. Hornbeam can help you get rid of any feeling of worry or procrastination. The flower essence Hornbeam is known to help increase your personal strength, motivation, and energy.

Conclusion

I hope this book was able to help you to identify a variety of ways that you can use to boost your own self-confidence so that you can live a happy, fulfilling, and successful life!

The next step is to start working on your foundation. Focus on exercising, eating healthy, mental exercises, and training yourself in the habits from Chapter 2. Once you've mastered your favorite habits, you can go back to the exercises from Chapter 3 and set some personal goals that can help boost your self-confidence. Starting with some short-term goals, work on them at home and at work until you have accomplished some long-term goals. Remember, you are worthy and deserving of only the best things in life! Live it well!

Finally, if you discovered at least one thing that has helped you or that you think would be beneficial to someone else, be sure to take a few seconds to easily post a quick positive review. As an author, your positive feedback is desperately needed. Your highly valuable five star reviews are like a river of golden joy flowing through a sunny forest of mighty trees and beautiful flowers! *To do your good deed in making the world a better place by helping others with your valuable insight, just leave a nice review.*

My Other Books and Audio Books
www.AcesEbooks.com

Health Books

Peak Performance Books

Be sure to check out my audio books as well!

 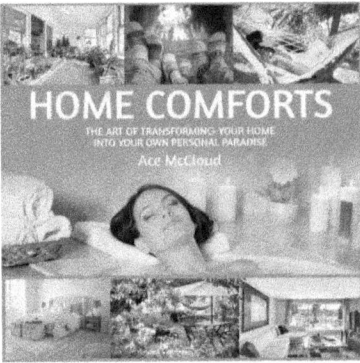 

Check out my website at: www.AcesEbooks.com for a complete list of all of my books and high quality audio books. I enjoy bringing you the best knowledge in the world and wish you the best in using this information to make your journey through life better and more enjoyable! **Best of luck to you!**

www.ingramcontent.com/pod-product-compliance
Lightning Source LLC
Chambersburg PA
CBHW051428070526
44584CB00023B/3627